CW01208041

Nick Burbridge

The Unicycle Set

First published in 2011
by Waterloo Press (Hove)
95 Wick Hall
Furze Hill
Hove BN3 1PF

Printed in Palatino 10.7pt by
One Digital
54 Hollingdean Road
East Sussex BN2 4AA

© Nick Burbridge 2011
All rights remain with the author.

Cover artwork 'Paper Circus' © Pia Bramley 2011
Cover design & Typesetting © Waterloo Press 2011

Nick Burbridge is hereby identified as author of this work in accordance with Section 77 of the Copyright, Designs and Patents Act 1988

This book is sold subject to the condition that it shall not, by way of trade or otherwise, be lent, resold, hired out or otherwise circulated without the author's prior consent in any form of binding or cover other than that in which it is published and without a similar condition including this condition being imposed on the subsequent purchaser.

A CIP record for this book is available
from the British Library

ISBN 978-1-906742-28-7

Acknowledgements

Thanks to the editors of the following journals and webzines where original versions of some of these poems have previously appeared: *Acumen, Agenda, Ambit, Assent, Envoi, Football Poets, The Frogmore Papers, Orbis, Other Poetry, Poetry Nottingham, the Recusant, Smith's Knoll, Spokes, Weyfarers, The Yellow Crane, Zeitriss.*

'Supper' was first published in the anthology *Emergency Verse — Poetry in Defence of The Welfare State,* (ed. Alan Morrison; Caparison 2010).

By the same author

Poetry
On Call (Envoi Poets Publications, 1994)
All Kinds Of Disorder (Waterloo Press, 2006)

Prose
Operation Emerald (as Dominic McCartan, Pluto, 1985)
War Without Honour (with Fred Holroyd, Harrap/Medium, 1989)

Plays
Neck/Cutting Room (Bright Red Theatre, 1987)
Vermin (Finborough Theatre, 1991)
Cock Robin (Brighton Festival, 1992)
Dirty Tricks (Soho Theatre, 1995)
Grosse Fugue (BBC Radio 4, 1995)
Scrap (South East Arts Tour, 1997)
Rites Of Passage (BBC Radio 4, 1999)

Albums
The Enemy Within (Hag Records, 1989)
World Turned Upside Down (Hag Records, 2001)
Claws And Wings (Hag Records, 2003)
Disorder (Hag Records, 2004)
Goodbye To The Madhouse (OTF Records, 2007)
All Kinds Of Disorder (M2H Records, 2008)
Besieged (M2H Records, 2011)

Contents

Unicycle	1
Animal, Vegetable, Or Mineral	2
As We Forgive Those…	4
Hamster	5
Rationalists	7
Under Wraps	8
Euphonium	10
Bipolar Expeditions	11
Solomon Baker's Report	13
Cappuccino	14
Half Empty Half Full	15
The Proud Uncle	16
Plec	17
Eamonn's Extraction	20
Where Were You When Obama Was Elected?	22
Christmas Eve	23
Actress	24
Dance No.6 Pt.2	25
Bad Medicine	27
Ludo	28
Mandolin Man	30
Alt. Folk Tale: The Flute Player's Lament	31
Monk's House	33
Private Ant	35
Summer Break	36
Impotence	37
Minutes	38
Connection	40
Murphy's Wake	41
Nihilists	43
Flynn's Budget	44
Six Minute Walk	46
Malloy As Cult Figure	47
Festival	49
Short Cuts	50
Alt. Folk Tale: The Demon Fiddler	52
On Guard	54
Mr O'Regan Calls Time	55

Artful Dodger	56
Rabbit	57
Nightlights	59
Mrs Malloy	60
S.O.S.	61
Park Life	62
Resurrection Reel	63
Herpes Variations	64
Godfather	65
Fringe Theatre	66
Trust Property	67
Talking Cure	69
Seeing Things Through	70
Little Mal	72
Malloy's Christmas Message	73
Soft Territory	74
Flynn's Christmas List	75
Tracks	76
Kiss Me Hardy	77
Groombridge	78
Malloy's Retreat	79
Terrapin	80
Envoi (The Stowaway's Song)	82

*For Martin, Gabriel, Tony, Niall,
fellow-travellers, moved on now*

Masters, you are fair, and you are true.
The world appears as brave as it is new.
For crumbs of comfort let us sing to you
Now we can't have our cake and eat it too.

('Supper')

The Unicycle Set

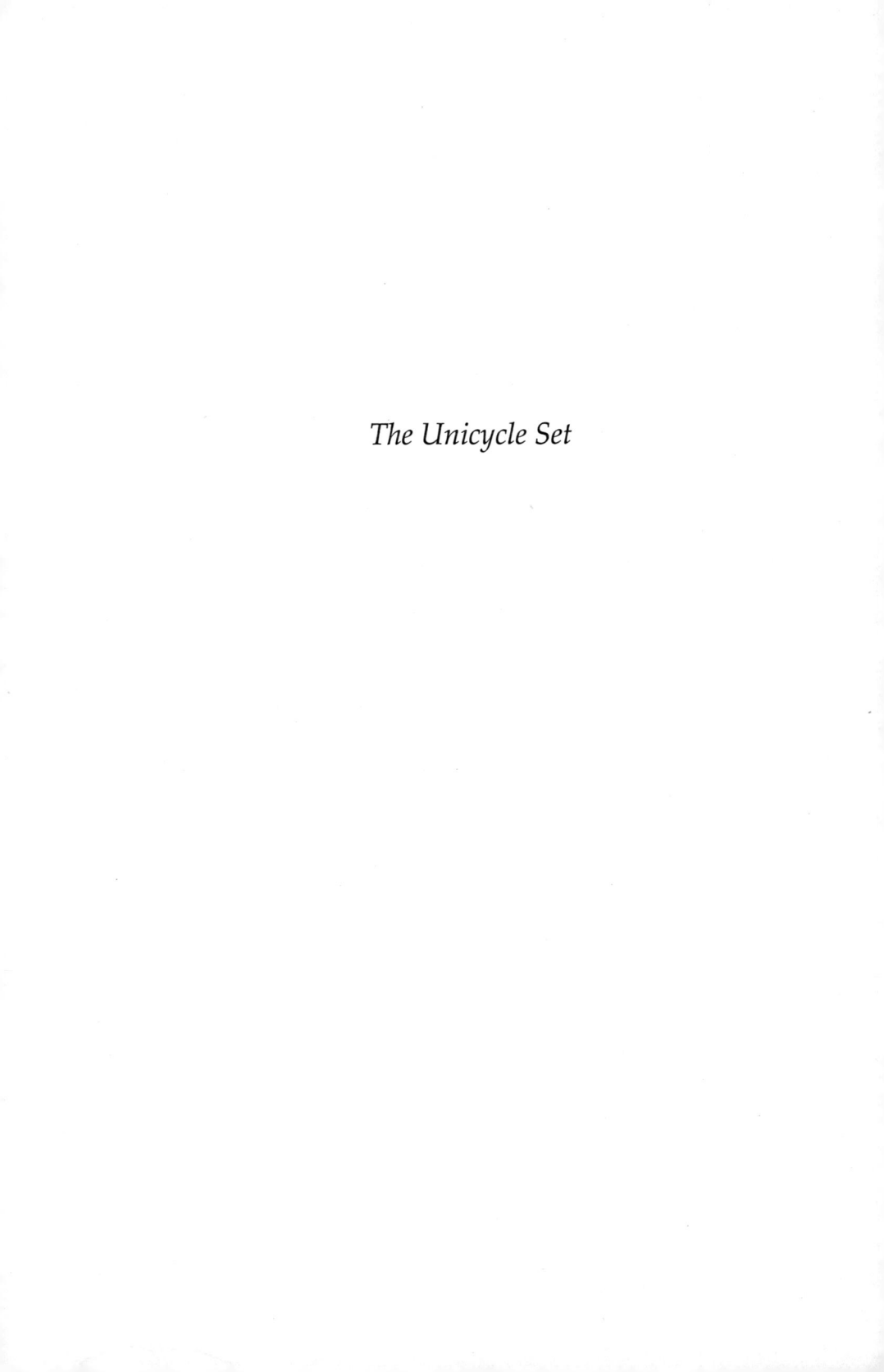

UNICYCLE

Street theatre makes Flynn weep.
The small boy on his shoulders
pins back chances of disguise
so he shuffles in sunshafts with soaked cheeks.
Take it at face value: bowed man, stunned
by what happens when jugglers and clowns
define spaces among hard grey surfaces,
phalanxes of strangers gather in the name of play,
glimpses what it might seem to be human
and recalls, with rue, how it becomes him.

Do not ask how many hours he sleeps
or with what substance; have him wax
on molten surges of adrenaline
that erupt in him, leave landscapes
obliterated by hard grey wastes of rock
constantly colliding with cold black tides
in his depths, where all bursts peter out.
Or worse, turn clever, talk re-uptake inhibitors;
in contrast to random raids,
clinical attacks of enemies within.

This is the moment when the straw-haired figure
on a unicycle flips spoon, cup and saucer
(not in that order) onto the crown of his head;
tomfoolery becomes heroic;
Flynn transforms the volcanic sob
which resonates in his son's gut
to a burst of laughter and applause.
Leave it at that: bathos of a bowed man
happy as Larry, whoever he is,
or, since he's long forgotten, Flynn.

ANIMAL, VEGETABLE, OR MINERAL

Five years to the royal telegram
if he can bear himself so far.
The mirror offers his lost form:
stooped shoulders, sitter's paunch,
sallow features scarred by falls.
He is the spit now of my brother,
near his end. He wouldn't know it.
He last saw him when he left him
on a closed ward, three years old.
But this is not unusual.
Once lost, such creatures
waited often unrecovered.

Soldier, to expatriate, he would repeat
cervecas por favor! — it's one thing he regrets.
He had good reasons: the prevailing climate,
lack of agencies, erosion of his other children.
On his only trip to the asylum some weeks later
he believed the boy's blunt brain denied him.
He determined it a kind of boarding school.
Perhaps he didn't know his son was left
rocking by his bed with dwarves and giants,
how local lads snuck through the grounds at dusk
to throw stones at barred windows,
listen to the animals bellow inside.

I don't deal in handicaps, or hold regrets.
I have prints that fix her exiled uncle years after
in my hearth, gap-toothed and bullet-headed,
touching fingers with my infant daughter,
wreathed in gases manufactured
from his turkey, sprouts, potatoes, parsnips.
Others, where he walked beside my teenage son
down a cloistered avenue of pines
to somewhere he alone imagined.
I still feel the dry press of his brow on mine
between swapped handfuls of soft sweets
in the half-hour visits we could both sustain.

A small brass plaque I ordered at his death
for the wood mount in our parish patch of rest
has no title in parentheses (say, vegetable)
to separate him from the solid citizens
with heads screwed on all round him.
Laying flowers with my own, it strikes me
the love of son and father renews always
in potential, like the love of brothers.
So however he defined his needs
this officer still at his glass should face charges
of desertion, if not crimes more serious,
though, in the act, I can't compare their loss.

I think that when both men are gone
to sulfur, cobalt, iron and other minerals,
they should be known by their farewells.
Urban crematorium, a blusterous May noon,
ward-mates hollering through hymns
reeling as coffin on rollers rocked.
Or a ceremony on some far Calvario,
tapestry of still or absent mourners,
military two-step, glittering stone cross.
Unless they are remembered here,
where one stares at the other with filmed eyes,
lame duck and ancient mariner, unrecognised.

AS WE FORGIVE THOSE…

Suave tongue and spread lips aside,
Fiddler Molloy recalls his lover Maia
for their rites of passage
in her seedy attic lodging.

Drunken inquisitions as they trailed back
through city streets, meant his secret was confessed.
She squatted on her bucket in the corner pissing.
He undressed her, penitently roused.

She covered him with tenderness.
Though they kicked a candle over
and suspended contortions to fight fire,
when at last he came across her breasts

(a stab at birth control)
fingering the limpid pools,
she said, 'It's time I was baptised';
wiped her brow and cheeks.

A Cork boy intimately schooled in Roman habits,
spent Malloy felt newly sanctified.
But when he left, for his now extant wife,
the landlady, old hippie in her kitchen

drinking herbal tea and licking a tahini jar,
met Maia's entrance (glistening face,
shift too short and torn,
to the uncommitted, smelling rank)

not as a celebrant — 'Three in a week' —
and wondered if she were
the lost and lonely tenant
she'd been led to believe.

Stepping from her tattered lamp-lit hall
into the dark night air,
Malloy stole homeward like a fox
barking sorrow and delight.

HAMSTER
Minor Miracle

Flynn, the unipolar man, through many childhoods
under house arrest, vicarious investor in small animals,
fostered his last daughter's hamster
when she took to handling other things.

For the senile Syrian, expectations had grown thin.
But Flynn cleared impacted pouches,
broke up cereal and nuts to fragments,
force-fed water from a spare syringe,
cleaned parts she could no longer reach.

Aside from stiff-limbed rambles on the bedspread,
nest-arranging, mounting plastic ramps,
she fed, slept, slept, fed, and was communed with.
Each evening, under his palm, she lay
against his heart, slumbering, as he leant back
in headphones, with a relaxation tape,
black cat in his lap to keep an eye on things.

Several weeks of unforeseen well-being.
Basking in the smell of him,
eyes keen and ears pinned,
she rediscovered the intent of scurrying,
turned circles before pissing in her place,
tumbled on her side, bicycled to right herself,
strewn with sawdust and fruit-peel, set off again.

When her spine irrevocably curled,
set to walk, she closed fawn lids and snored,
Flynn sought to cultivate detachment like a hospice nurse.
But, glimpsing a dark form beneath the ladder
splayed, wide-eyed and cold, it left him.

Rodent bones litter the backyard bed.
Flynn could not dispose of her; he cradled her,
rigid, by his heart, into the living room, and stared
through distance glasses shielding his wet eyes.
So there were witnesses. Minutes passed before
her limbs began to twitch, they heard her rasp.

Breath took to her lungs, and persevered,
although her eyes stayed wide and black.
Her heart danced uncertainly, she softened and unbent.
His first delight turned to a meddling sense of guilt.
But, as his family stared at him, she squealed three times
in anguish and farewell, arched, fell; vindicated him.

Another corpse was buried in the backyard mausoleum.
At Christmas, no one bought a pup
of gnawing expectations and a passion to revolve.
Old age approached him like an outsized cartoon rat.

So Flynn paddles past his daughter's room,
peers in at the empty cage, as if it will be full;
sits in his grey chair with ear-phones and black cat,
wandering wild scented gardens.

But instead of settling to focus on a sleeping form
where all grew still and needed of him
only a warm palm, heartbeat, familiar smell,
his mind careers among cages of his brood,
climbing captive bars, treading racks and wheels.
It is what crucifies dark Flynn, or so he thinks.
By all means laugh at him. But he can raise
small rodents from the dead. That's more than some.

RATIONALISTS

Irrigators are despondent.
Dust has blown for years
into their eyes
but their own tears are redundant.

Dam buildings decay.
They dream of millwheels and glaciers,
while ditches become graves
where ants forage for leaves.

Their bones will bleach here.
They invest all they have.
Sources still weep,
freely, underground.

UNDER WRAPS

In my brown-and-white Hollywood dream
you call from a phone-box by the pocked ice-track's
artery that runs through densely loaded pines.
The operator lures me from the rocking-chair.
I leap into a Ford truck with snow-chains,
the scenery starts to rush past.

At the far end of track-marks I find you
at your last gasp — torn brown leather
turned to a white cocoon, littered by fresh needles.
Freeze-frame: I hold you to my breast
like a poor man's James Stewart.
Christmas bells over the closing scene:
snowballs thrown, not fixed into your vein.

You cut your own high-definition Brighton rock.
Silhouetted among swirls of summer dust
in moonlight by the West Pier ruins.
Call up one of the pock-cheeked couriers
who cross the city on pushbikes.
Then get followed to a dealer's,
as dawn breaks, busted by the snatch squad,
wraps stashed between your cheeks.

Out on bail and codeine, tell me
only when you turn up in the paper.
Fade down slowly as you drop from a back window,
meet another messenger beneath park willows
and shoot up; always one good lie from being found.

Bad news. These are shelved scripts.
All roads to the wood are blocked.
You used to shudder at Hansel and Gretel;
you are the little match-girl now.
There, by the sea's plash, blades are out,
pigs are bent; in so deep, you could go down.

Perhaps, on some day to come,
a poor man's Billingham will call for a few shots:
council flat, ankle tag, piles of DVDs,
rain on the window, cans and works.
And you'll have this, blue-toothed from my phone —
self-portrait, knees bent and hands clasped —
Subject: *Old Man Praying*. All that's left to cut.

EUPHONIUM
Brighton 2009

Now look. Tuba player on stilts
in the Pavilion Gardens, running through
Stravinsky, Monty Python,
Benny Hill in hot pursuit.

Give a tenner for the convoluted instrument —
despite the art of buzzing lips
and the sanction of great ears —
that summons ferry boats and flatulence.

And another for the neatly-timed accompaniment
to Rombouts and rock-cake, late September afternoon
before the drunks take seats for the dusk train;
like dead letters, wraps change hands.

As the giant spits into his squashed trombone
while city stalwarts fill his upturned hat:
gay old cruiser with his Shitz Tsus,
macho poser, bare torso and T'ai Chi moves,

plump rouged tart and Dali clone on wheels —
crumpled melancholic armed with twenty notes —
mark this heart, top of the misuse charts, for all it is.
Horn-filled circus. Cod palace. Excess charge. Burlesque.

BIPOLAR EXPEDITIONS

Midnight's gone, your phone's live
by the bed; you recoil from me;
sleep retreats, as a missed tide.
It's high time; she's running naked
through her neighbour's rooms,
squatting in their baths and showers,
howling about storms and model boats.

Poles apart, you plot with unseen ministers
one more passage to the locked ward,
surf for timetables, rooms, tickets,
arrange cover, assess the home's in hand.
No mother could deny her.

Yet in a few weeks when confinement bites,
the scattergun of chemicals brings down
insurgents leaping her mind's gaps,
captive anger kowtows to common sense,
she shuffles in her corner and mumbles
about drowning as she yields to waves of sleep —

you will change tack, angle for release dates,
care-plans, crash-teams, home-tutors,
curse her somnolence; urge adrenalin,
which arms her now, to come in peace
and drive her reconstruction,
trust again that this time is the last.

Such navigation wearies you.
So I turn empty-handed to the dark
while you lie half-awake, listening to coastal reports,
as if the bestowal of such names means
waves will not erode the rocks round Mallin Head,
nor sandbanks build invisibly by Dover Straits.

But on the causeway you become between steep cliffs,
true as any field you might have her wander,
you must shield her from the worst falls
and, if she grows numb, cruelly start her.
Meanwhile, needs of others fill this house;
you must wait, temperately, till she calls.

SOLOMON BAKER'S REPORT

Solomon Baker laughs too much,
saddled with the fool's part.
He can fake-fart in each crook and crack,
peel back eyelids, gurn like a yokel;
has sharp wits, a filthy tongue,
reams of jokes off the wall.
I think he is cause for concern.

There's an open secret, long vouchsafed to him,
his birth-mother flew off Beachy Head
only weeks after his entrance.
While life with his adopted parents —
a Marxist reconstructed as town hall executive
and his shy wife, fluent in four languages —
is laced with many benefits:

each day he dips into this legacy
racked by fear and anger he can't articulate,
which proves not all things are so risible.
Yet he conceals the evidence,
laughing on street corners, school buses,
along corridors, in classes and photographs.

It is not my job to rear him
but I've known him since his first smile.
I hear his father has a furious bowel;
his mother, gone off the rails.
I should warn him of the years ahead
peppered with test sheets and pigeon-holes
when laughter might be detrimental.

I will corner him one evening in the park
playing what begins as football
but turns into wrestling and devilry:
Solomon, life is hell sometimes
and must be handled with a decent strategy.
Yet not before I've witnessed his full repertoire —
and if I do not howl — for he knows this all too well.

CAPPUCCINO

You caught sight of her last week,
as you set off to feed crusts to badgers,
arm in arm with her fellow-traveller,
stealing away from park toilets.

What they do there
is marked by debris,
traces of gear, hard scars
on their soft flesh pressed together.

Yet every time you meet her
over a table where cups gather,
shame and fury disappear
like froth; you back off,

haunted by the slip who darted
among trees in sunlight, caught the flag,
skipped and leapt into your lap,
on a safe bench with her book-bag.

Who is this feral one
with burnt-out eyes and sores?
She needs all you give. Leave,
or you lose all you have.

HALF EMPTY HALF FULL

After his T'ai Chi class at the Friends' centre
John the filing clerk, buoyed by inner energies
forging through channel and gate,
feels ready to trespass on territory
avoided with timidity
to stand his ground
in harmony and strength.

Waiting for his Calibur with a low centre,
he inspects the bowed hulk at the bar.
Just this morning Cork McShane was laid off
from the docks, and his wife left him
with the children and her lover's gonorrhea;
so when John's inquiry on the status of his glass
intrudes into his thoughts, a taut line snaps.

Scarred and florid with mop of curls
meets aquiline pale pursed in a smile.
Neither remembers the next moment — nor even
the precise movement, which baulks no block;
only how the glass butts and explodes
on the one side, with a vent of venom;
on the other, a concussive blast.

The detached observer might pursue the metaphor
among fragments lodged in the clerk's skull,
pools of Guinness mingling with blood
as the docker stares into a black hole
where his future collapses like a squeezebox
playing a reel he hasn't even heard
yet knows suddenly by heart.

But while the perfect regularity of breath,
still limbs and quietly parted lips,
through the next months in coma,
might seem echoes of a meditative state,
John no longer cares what angle
to come at things, if mind and matter merge.
It just pays to know what happens next.

THE PROUD UNCLE

Six months after
their daughter's still-birth
his sister
has a healthy girl.

He resolves to lie low
for some weeks at least
but Facebook profiles
fill with photographs.

He posts "how beautiful she is!"
and visits
on a rose-filled evening in June.
His wife pleads migraine.

When he holds the child
he appears to dissolve
as if suspended
in a spiritualist shot.

But he will not part
with her. Between the ghost
pressed to his breast
and the quick shape in his grip

he draws breath.
And he is redefined;
although it is not clear
if he weeps in joy or grief.

PLEC

Flynn's wife had from her reclusive man
an algae-eater for the hall aquarium,
bulging eyes, swift tail, puckered snout
to fix himself to rocks and glass, and suck.

Although he only hoovered slime
he grew at an uncanny rate and soon resembled
a thin yellow penis, half-erect but deftly tapered,
so he shuffled back into his cave under the pump

then swished around the tank,
curled and twirled, breakneck, without malice
but with fatal consequences to stray shoals,
and adhered like a sentry while he fed.

One evening, when her husband had retired
to ward off predators,
she spied the algae-eater, stoutly swollen,
wedged between the stanchions

of the ornamental bridge.
Expert teacher in Linguistics,
but no dab-hand
in aquatic signs,

she was swept through by panic.
Gentle pulls and prods ignored,
she put the bridge into a bowl of water,
took a hacksaw to the ledge,

shook it, tried to snap it,
and, unlike her, swore.
With thumb and forefinger
she tried manoeuvring it back and forth.

His silence as he watched her, panting,
made her weep.
But with one sudden flick
he quivered and shot free.

Tipped into the tank, he lingered by the pump
for several days, gills like bellows,
ventured a few circles, fastened to the glass,
gave an imitation of fair health.

But where his slime-coat had been damaged,
when he took up bed-disturbing journeys
filth soon mottled him,
microbes rushed in.

Hours in a self-willed maelstrom
wounding several rasbora
left him lying at the front
where, eyes on hers, he expired.

She tried to flush him to the sewers
but he wedged in the water
like an animated turd
so she slipped him in the wheelie bin.

Experts in the fish shop told her
algae-eaters in tight spots
inflate to put off predators;
had she left him in the darkness

he would have squirmed free.
She informed Flynn. 'Extend this
to the U-bend and his mortal soul,'
he said. 'I'm not replacing him.'

So in the morning, cradling her coffee cup,
or after work, too tired to lift it up,
she stands in her hallway
watching ornate guppies, robust tetra,

wishing only the ugly algae-eater
still eyed her from his cave, would snip-
-snap through the water and adhere
to the glass, disguised as a thermometer —

for a beautiful and clever woman,
an odd place to be in. But who to blame?
Plecostomus or Flynn?
Thirty years to answer. She may now begin.

EAMONN'S EXTRACTION

The local middle class adored him,
like the new plumber who promises
to redeem past errors;
he filled his waiting room
with wide-eyed families,
worked two chairs at once,
skipping to each surgery,
his well-worn patter
setting ridden minds at rest
on root canal, amalgam, empty gum.

But when the plot collapsed
they dug out different scripts.
I only kept one cut,
shot through amitriptyline.
He was so desperate *tic douloureux*
should be some dental pain,
he pulled an innocent premolar.
Forceps cracked the rim. When our eyes collided
I could see a torn black nerve, long since exposed in me,
but in my dentist I would rather not have hit.

Rumours spread of gambling, sickness,
fist-fights with his alcoholic father;
infidelity with nurses, threats from his wife,
high-flying in obstetrics, to leave him with the children.
Yet, through part-song of precision instruments
and local radio he kept building bridges,
tapped on crowns, made humdrum stabs and scrapes.
Pulling foam plugs from my daughter's gums
and snapping his paper mask, *That's It Now*,
from his lips, still set fears to rest.

When he was late for dinner one November evening
his new widow broke into the surgery to find him
dangling from the balcony, still in tunic and trainers.
Seven hundred mourners filled St Mary Magdalene
to sing his requiem, mouths open, filled and cleaned by him.
But, as his coffin bobbed and veered from sight
no echoes of his own assurance followed him,
just one cry only from his mother, a refrain
perhaps he heard too often as he cut his own milk teeth:
Jesus, Eamonn, now what have you done?

WHERE WERE YOU WHEN OBAMA WAS ELECTED?

'78, it was all Red Theatre,
happenings in the street, fretless bass,
mushrooms, modules on Baader Meinhoff;
above all, hatred of the States.

Now he meets me between flights
from LA to Abu Dhabi, with the opera.
Green gumboots for Glastonbury; sharp suits
for party and convention: jim@safeevents.com.

This isn't a complaint; the lineaments
of constructive middle-age
sit better with his rotund shape
than tight black t-shirts and clenched fists;

a leveller's need to crash barriers
quietly replaced by the acumen
to build them, whoever pays him,
whatever tickets cost.

Sage men move with the times;
agitprop and rhetoric
swapped for the safety of structures
above, below, and behind them.

But, for all his new-found status,
I have yet to hear him say
one black face in the gantry
makes the theatre a safe place.

CHRISTMAS EVE
For Martin

As stained glass fades through the dusk
crib lights burnish; in his makeshift pen
by the confessional, a donkey shits.
Pews that dull Sundays leave void
billet bright-eyed families
armed with candles in card skirts.
The church curtseys for its happy hour.

After the first anthems, creaking up
and rustling down, the Sunday School nativity,
half-remembered lines and pre-recorded riffs
led by a pink fairy bopping by the pulpit.
For his sermon the priest takes Joseph,
swathes him in paper and gaffer tape.
When he emerges we sing Happy Birthday Jesus.
Prayers are to be bubbles blown from a pot,
but through weak lungs or heating cuts
they drop at his feet on the stone steps, pop.

And yet, so restive is our trapped urge,
hush and shadows cast by candle-flame
for the communion make some
appear transfigured,
like Sassoon's stuck soldier,
by the shaft of an almighty answer.
It's just a trick of the light.

The circus rolls to an end.
The faithful are not called to come,
but anyone, in choruses
more vaudeville than Jerusalem.
Children shuffle in litter by the stable
torn between horseplay and sanctimony.
Bells collide. Sole sticks to sud.
As he shakes hands on the steps outside
the vicar warms to his next sacrament:
print tablecloth, mince pies, mulled wine.

ACTRESS

Look out. Lush in the red velvet bar
holding forth to dancers from Aladdin
at the Royal; trench coat, long locks,
cocked hat, white wine and Gauloises,

cast her as her own stage manager
on these stained boards,
leading lady in a melodrama
slugged out over fifty years

so wherever you come in,
eavesdroppers that you are,
sin and corpse surround her.
Can you blame her if she twists

the plot *(oh yes you can!)* that stifles her
like creeping damp — fear of failure,
memory of shock — and steals
each scene by dying on her feet?

Young hopefuls, catch her later
when she falls. I owe her little now
but, in the name of acts we laboured at,
I would not see her cut.

DANCE N0.6 PT.2

When Dick's drunk at dinner with our friends
the set-designer and his potting partner
he takes off down the road to the local diva's house
(while reviews hail him as a modern dance master)
and stands in the gutter, shouting:
'You tosspot, you poser,
come out here, I loathe you!'
And when no one appears to challenge him
goes back to the table, satisfied, victorious.

Dick sculpts in a small way.
A few years ago he watched his wife beat cancer,
only to fly through the windscreen,
fatally, one early summer morning
on the way to Cornwall.
His son has some problems with behaviour.

But he is not alone.
As I pass the diva
walking his dogs in the park,
bald head and earrings,
goatee, shades and swagger,
I swear at him under my breath.

In a similar period
I lost my brother in an epileptic fit
and my obese daughter walked out.
Like Dick, I mess with forms,
obscurely. We are both blunted.
His knife remains sharper.

The diva's latest show sees him
give a breathtaking performance
among dripping ice cubes
to a unique electronic score,
fully funded, sold out,
and booked for a long tour.

His is a handsome house,
he has two presentable children,
and, presumably, a troupe of lovers.
Should a seminal creator
be the butt of so much vitriol?
I don't know the answer.
But, in this city,
Dick and I are not unusual.
Some men make you want to spit.

BAD MEDICINE

The Moon Bear slips
into a nightmare
where they force
him to dance.

When he wakes
the barbed shunt
in his gall-bladder
bites and aches.

Under the cage
bile drips into
a tray, destined
for the phial.

Dancing would be
a kind of fate,
pit-fighting,
taking bait.

Here he drains, only,
wrestles his own pain.
His eyes close slowly.
No more trance.

LUDO

The first time a long throw takes you clear
the Japanese are laying tracks across Burma,
you leave your lacemaker in a London store,
sending dockets on cylinder and wire —
nursing the daughter you will see no more —
and in camouflage and officer's moustache
take the soulful nurse who tends your scars,
as she will now for thirty years;
or, so you write home, hitch your wagon to the stars.

Sad to see it parked up on a suburban lawn
peeled and faded by decades of fake peace,
you on a daily pilgrimage to the ministry,
she hemmed in by hypochondria,
and growing among lupins and dahlias
a dry spread of weeds.
Sadder still the offspring you have barked
into form, straying in the wilderness,
so you slow-march under your sycamores,
as if to seek out why,
but quietly covet the next man's grass,
peel your wandering eye.

Before old age traps you with their broods
your cup spills and you cut free
to the Spanish mountains
with a ballroom dancer,
shuffle off suit and bowler, layers of pale skin,
grandsons and daughters, for her sweat and sangria;
and with the ruptured appetite of autumn
roll in her lap, your helpmate, your lost earth,
each hot step stretching the distance you have breached
only by acceptably penned letters;
your relief and happiness proof
that to advance well is to learn how to retreat.

So when the sap falls, the sun turns to a threat,
you slope back to shelter in the Mendips,
your last moves only for cream teas and shopping trips.
Eyes fail, and you collide with supermarket doors.
Legs fail, and a dance of bloody falls
leads you to the last armchair, swathed like a child,
raging against mobile, laptop, the age of digital:
tunnels we might dig to you,
your ministering angel keeps blocked.

The last exit lies at the next turn
and when the cup tips you have to take it,
leaving the unopened and deleted lost.
This should be the hour of forgiveness.
So why does some heretic text you in the night hours
when echoes of our lives still reach you
so you have to listen to the landline robot?
hey, hows u? heard ur weak but wats nu?
from all us u hav left, 4 all the times u failed us, thanx.
A pettiness. And you will not reply.
But I wanted you to get the message, now,
before I'm jumped and have to start again, you die.

MANDOLIN MAN
Koan

Focus, for a moment, on the left hand.
Though the other seems to have command,
it marks time, juggles with triplets and upbeats,
yet serves what constantly unwinds.

These are the slender fingers that transport
signals from the pure tracts of the heart.
Stab or linger, in descant or descent,
they lead out what's coded in the instrument.

Sun that strikes an unknown busker's back
bowed over the carved bowl curled in his lap,
while he conjures with the ornamented neck,
strikes your creased brow as you break step.

Listen. This is why — for you are curious,
although you don't remember what it is you ask —
even a line of unravelled silence
is a gift you shouldn't shun.

Walk on. It drifts behind you without moving.
The levelling sun surrounds you still;
at your point of rest, in a hand full of intent,
what may be made resounds, what may be meant.

ALT. FOLK TALE: THE FLUTE PLAYER'S LAMENT

Back off tour, Malloy's to the pub for a lock-in.
But the local Highland Piper, in full gear,
lurches from the bar, cups his ear and whispers:
'Your wee flute-player. Meningitis. Did you hear?'

It seems he walked into this scene before,
but reeling at its senselessness,
Malloy weighs impulse with restraint.
Whiskey has him leave his instruments,
and takes him through the drizzling city streets
to landmark towers, the sanctum of Intensive Care,
lilts his true tale of adultery so sadly
to the night nurse, she swaps propriety
for film scene, and lets him pass.

Luck meets him. Family at home, to rest
before the final watch, his lover lies alone
as some freak Millais might have had her
fingers touching at her breast,
still white and soft-skinned
among drones and regulators.
Lips once pursed at the flute
harbour the coarse tube that mimics breath
her fingers used to turn to silk
as they skipped along the stops
on *The Connaught Man's Rambles*.
Though these instruments keep perfect time
they bear a woman burdenless.

No sense comes until the light of day.
So Malloy leaves home, with a new set of lies.
At the doorway to a separate white room,
he meets a husband and his daughter grieving.
In innocence, they clasp him as a family friend.
His lover's metronomic rest is at an end.
Unplugged from lines and lights
she's discoloured, cold and still.
He bends to kiss her brow, watches

as the girl cleaves to her, breast to breast.
Her body arcs with grief. Her shirt lifts.
He sees her mother's flesh
and swears himself to silence.

Yet, driven by undying need
he vows, when this has passed —
staring from van windows at unwinding miles,
taking others to expunge her
or playing the good father —
he will take her to his lips, and on some distant stage
where other lines and lights transfigure time,
silken, warm and pliant, as she came to him,
together they will play her true lament.

MONK'S HOUSE
via Ashdown Forest

Patient and poetaster, Flynn,
had to piss on the outing
which ended at Monk's House.

By the outdoor closet
he waited for
a constipated tourist

ten minutes
till he reappeared,
tucked his floral shirt

into his shorts,
and confessed,
'It's kinda blocked.'

Flynn used the basin
but curiously flushed
and stood awash.

At the house he wiped his feet,
stepped into the vestibule
and, like a boy, gasped.

A pair of brown boots,
rain-hat
and walking-sticks

stood as if left
that morning: spares
for Mrs Woolf.

The stone bust
on the garden wall
induced a dizzy spell.

'Against you, I will fling myself

unvanquished and unyielding, o death!
…The waves broke on the shore…'

The wind sighed through the elm.
In the valley the Ouse plashed.
A train to Lewes hooted.

Flynn turned to his shadow:
'Does my trouble lie
in trying to digest

a smackerel
of some gift, or curse, like this,
across the years?'

He got short shrift:
'Possession of notebook
and anorak is a recipe

for spotting trains.
Driving complex engines
through heaven and hell

(let me be tactful)
calls for infinitely
better skills —

and, don't forget,
hours and conditions
infinitely worse.'

Flynn grinned. 'Medication,'
said his shadow. They joined hands
and danced across the grass.

PRIVATE ANT

The monk-like old man whom others in the altar army
christened Private Ant, on his way to morning Mass
blacked out and fell like a shot squaddie,
skull on stone, blood in animated coils.
At the margins of his pilgrimage
along the Roman road, he listened to his sins squawk,
aching to confess. But, coming to, *pieta*,
at a woman's breast, he glimpsed the barren rafters
of the Quaker Meeting House he had been passing.
And no dance of numbed limbs could transport him.

Among echoes and dark swirls he heard a distant voice:
round another bend there stood St Matthew's
and the Anglicans at least. *Mea culpa...*
It had always been his failure: to reach where he was called —
the death-bed of his penitent and birdlike sister,
or the cottage of his undercover lover (hirsute shoulders,
foreskin of such tender folds), so many family red letters
dodged with migraine and fever —
for some privacy essential to his faith: or funk.
He vowed, if he survived, all things must change.

But — helped by Samaritans to his sick-bed,
wedded to machines by coils
and put back on his feet with stent
and rattling tubs — did Private Ant transform?
Like a lame duck on a dark stream he was borne;
while watchers on the bank asked what God would trade
the yield of ardent years for the hoard of a meek heart;
how a man with love to burn, conscience worked like bellows,
trembled through his fear of flame; if, even at the altar
where he knelt, he would be forgiven when he fell for good?

SUMMER BREAK

After maniacal days when the whiteboard walked out
and wheels fell off cardboard vehicles
ranged along class shelves, the bank of rest;
he came-to in a maize maze, an old game
hunting his children, cobs from cover aimed to miss.
But hunters had changed places; armed with mobiles
plotting ambush; so he raced along the aisles
edged in fear, till, at the heart, sun fell on him,
he ached so stubbornly for some lost stasis;
he would not move, even when cluttering husks
cracked his head, drew blood, and prompted
his son's voice: *He's not playing now.*

Blue August days; half-way to a new campaign.
Late nights at the screen with glasses of red wine,
planning his attacks, long mornings lost in bed,
drove him to the beach scene; clawing at what freed him
when he dug sand cars and castles once,
walked the bleached strand with his daughter,
last-born sleeping under an umbrella,
wife splayed nearby. But that moment
steeped in the forgiving sun — when all he made
he watched dismantled by the waves at play —
was hidden now by dark relentless passages,
or, as the small one cried: *The tide's already in.*

Bruised clouds massed at sea, forked and cracked.
At the first hiss and spit shingle cleared haphazardly.
Three wise monkeys squatted in his skull.
Raising the old brolly, clothes piled on his flesh
he sat cross-legged as the storm broke
in banks of hail on shingle cheeks,
until hours later when a posse had been gathered
and tough arms in green lifted his silhouette
from the stone line, facing the immeasurable.
Where he next came-to, as autumn settled in,
among new desks, beds, and corridors
he stood mumbling: *Do the terms here end?*

IMPOTENCE
'A rare event!' Flynn, Arctic Explorer

Equipped for explorations
along smooth white paths
to the magnetic pole, synapses strike;
crevasses surround Flynn, and he wilts.

Delusion — when his head detaches
like a space-pod, and looks down on the earth —
where he appears in discombobulating cameos:
Flynn's is his father's nakedness,

disappointingly small penis glimpsed
in chlorine-scented cubicles, behind beach towels,
roused obscenely. Man with brolly and buffed hat
uncurls as hirsute animal

for *Paso Doble* with his brittle mother
or the languid lover that he swaps her for.
And, no, is this Flynn's daughter, in her rites of passage,
leaping like a salmon from a crack between his legs?

Flynn squats by the bed-head
and bangs with both fists
in search of a lost medium:
is anybody there?

No one hears. This is the lap-land
of his nights, ice-caps that freeze sleep,
bedevilled by the northern lights.
Forgive him if he turns back.

MINUTES
Fellowship of Depressives Anonymous, 23rd June

Eight o'clock, at the main man's top floor flat
in a Regency building near St Michael's Church.
The tea-set ritual. First brew, formalities.
The failed Irish writer arrives late.
No one complains. Assembly on the three-piece suite.
Ten minutes each to navigate the week's depths
clears the second pot. To lubricate the free-for-all:
a last dance round the kettle. Introduction of the biscuit tin.

So the one-time teacher on a hot evening —
t-shirt, sawn-off denims — marshals his quartet.
The thin pale widow, tugging her stained roll-neck,
lists failed sallies to the shops and yields
to the postgraduate — impenetrable lenses and thick beard —
with medical snippets from radio and library books.
While the Dubliner, fresh from a Section unvisited,
picks up *The Sun* and eulogises on bare breasts.

No one objects. Order is kept at all costs.
Moments when it crashed are not forgotten.
Christmas, when the student's sausage-rolls uncurled,
serotonin raised by punch, he groped the widow,
on the stairs, fell and broke his ankle.
Or the evening in spring when the Dubliner announced
he had downed a pack of Prozac, but as help was called,
danced a jig and bellowed 'APRIL FOOL'.

They settle as the main man, unaware
his left testicle protrudes, leans back with eyes closed
to take elegantly phrased passages through hell.
Flooded with fatigue,
he watches his mind drift, dreaming
he has turned the helpline message on its head:
*Welcome to the FDA. If you're looking for support,
forget it, we've gone home to bed.*

No one bridles when he snorts. Through open windows
pigeons in the crescent trees compete
with Wimbledon highlights borne on the breeze.
This is as close as they come to peace.
Curfew is at ten. No one wants to leave.
So the Dubliner cavorts: 'May God go with you!'
And they go alone. The tea-set's washed,
hidden for another week. Like them.

CONNECTION

The back door opens.
A teenage girl
comes home,
to visit

so her stepfather —
head teacher
on extended leave —
peers between

the banisters, broken
as he sees himself
caress her breasts
with his palms,

sink his face
between her thighs,
mark the cotton
folded in her bag.

He retreats to his study
to assess the news:
another hunter
and a summer's kill.

He whispers
fiercely:
'Disconnect,
disconnect'…

How many steps
are there
to the patio,
unguarded?

MURPHY'S WAKE

In a cold meeting room at the Lake Motel
in the suburbs, Murphy has his poor man's memorial.
Swan-necked daughters, taught from childhood
to meet his excess with propriety,
lay out cups and saucers, copies of his memoirs.
On the covered table their starched mother
opens an old photograph of someone long divorced.
It looks like a miniature school Speech Day.
Not a jug of porter, even the hint of a jig.

Chlorine drifts from the rundown indoor pool.
Among the sombre-suited ranks
swimmers he had cornered
with his blarney in the sauna
summon the same restless humour
for his literary friends
and their carefully penned paeans
of baffled rue and blunt regard for him,
sleeper, and outsider, even among them.

Cut to a frost-struck morning days before.
At the mortuary I stand waiting with others
in the press-gang for these pale women.
The card coffin — Murphy's name scrawled on,
bumped out on a trolley, slid into a people-carrier —
climbs the short hill to the furnace in the woods.
Mourners unexpected, the sullen lad sweeps up,
the MC puts on Pachelbel's Canon
(I half-hear Murphy humming)

we are told how to bear him, left right left.
The feel of his form so sparely shielded
pulls my cheek against the fake board —
then we lay him, crooked, on the runners.
Given moments for our memories to gather,
we all sit at angles, picturing him bleutered
in his cabin-bed, bladder like a wine-skin split,
bleeding from half-hearted cuts: drying out
at last, since none of us discovered him for days.

[41]

Reverie splits reverie; my wife's hand falls
on mine, to prompt another obloquy.
But we took turns so often at lost soul and lifeguard,
to miss his sailor's grip makes no sense.
So I recall how he likened his own life
to a mouthful of bad teeth, aching to be filled
or pulled out once and for all.
I'd like to say this rings a bell for me,
but, like himself, goes down limply at the Lake Motel.

NIHILISTS

Tired of all we had arranged
we pulled the flowers, scoured the vessel,
stripped the prospect.

So we face the hard world
which makes us hard.
Lovers of emptiness.

Consider the crashed bowl now,
pulps of broken petals.
Isn't it time

to return it to the sun
splashed with colours?
Nakedness is more than this.

There are still shoots in the yard.
The drone of bees.
A hint of summers to come.

FLYNN'S BUDGET

Summer afternoons with patched rug and basket
when his mother's features bubble and contort
among the lineaments of others, family man Flynn
finds his picnic is again a sandwich short.

Cue Freudian fandangos,
interiors in an adrenal wash,
where doll's house walls, unfounded, shudder,
toy chandeliers of childhood crash…

Wasp scene. When the kitchen sanctum is invaded.
View from the wash-pile on all fours
while the porcelain one skips and slaps,
strips naked, is obscenely stung.

Early morning tea-tray dropped deliberately
downstairs. View from a cracked bedroom door:
the curtsey of failed legs that will perhaps propel
the weeping heap where smashed sets lie.

Ground floor occupied by local bourgeoisie
intent on frolics. View between two banisters:
the hostess, in her scent and jewellery, at ease,
although she sways discreetly, regal vowels slur.

Small hours, broken silence; her repression turns to fury;
for no reason Flynn can know but pledges to resolve.
Next morning, like dead fireworks, inspect lipstick
on the tips of Consulate and whisky rims.

Skip to the last reel. Smog-filled street. Flynn, at three,
with suitcase (spy camera POV) searching for some theatre
where the cast of *Your Life In Their Hands* perform
a hysterectomy that he alone can stop — he cannot stop…

Flynn lifts the basket with the same white-knuckled grip
and heads for shelter. There's a bent old doll
in a care home just along the coast
who does not fall, or dance at all now.

He's neglected her for years — and why?
He can't afford exteriors. This is her inheritance,
like all her precious ornaments,
occasionally buffed but never handled. Him.

SIX MINUTE WALK
For Aisling

Often — there is no good reason —
from elements at work or war
a force breathes pain, like poison,
into the lives of the callow
while the roughshod stalk and howl
through the night, unwounded.

If it strikes, you can't draw breath
under its influence,
and all it damages, in streams
that bear life through you, becomes debris;
you grow desolate, and waste the hours
asking why it is you cast apart.

Yet it is true, other streams
through our hearts run, inviolable.
If it brings comfort, picture their emblem
as a pure man pierced by thorn and nail,
or if it makes sense, look for this only
in the staunch eyes of the beloved.

Unbearably light, though in sorrow
making the heart so heavy,
where it breathes we are not broken
or undone, but our lives
like bruised lambs bursting stained sacs,
draw in the clear air of spring, renewed.

MALLOY AS CULT FIGURE

They have eaten me piecemeal through the years,
garnished with dry mushroom harvests,
dusted in unending wraps of coke,
washed down with breweries of Bushmills.
I'm lost somewhere in the shared gut
that bounces as they mosh and pogo
while incessant lines fixed from me
course around their hearts.

I wander my own chambers, I'm cleaned out.
My children pass me like strangers.
Their mother left me long ago to mobile numbers
across Europe; if services don't come
on a tour bus, I still use them. What else is there?
I vowed to walk the Galway coast,
but I came back in days, tired of my own hand,
coursed by the sound of emptiness.

To be so caught brooks no release;
the more the shadow protests,
the faster the fixed image sticks.
I trawl through evidence of many years,
stage shows and interviews — a rogue priest
full of litanies and fixed moves —
to find innocence. There is none.
To dodge the weeks between rushes
I take my old box and torn throat
to caverns for the core hundreds.
There the dregs at least get sucked.

I don't want to come here — backstreet pub
in the bleak hours after a sound-check —
where you circle your winter fire,
growing old together with new songs,
still mining a hard day's seam
but reaching for the valve that draws clear air.
You eye me at the bar before the stage calls.
Believe me, it grows cold there.

Dry ice, strobe lights, snare drum and bass riff
sign a warning I no longer hear,
so hollow is my ear, empty the form I dance to it.

FESTIVAL

Grim Flynn the busker and his shadow
muttering like cronies on his pitch
beneath Max Miller's plinth as the parade files past
hit on an old mucker with a djembe in the Samba Troupe.

Shaved skull and spectacles, trance-smile and overalls,
stalwart of green politics and loving-kindness,
his mind full of rhythms from Lagos to Dun Laoghaire,
he comes whistling like a one-man Radhakhrishna band.

Yet he has trials. His father calls him ineffectual.
His first wife left him for another woman
and took half their child. Viruses keep occupying forces
in his glands. His *Fusion* magazine has been hit hard.

But, says shade to Flynn, regard the man you cannot be
and don't deride him. Cry *Arriba* and *Oi Vay!*
You're just a bum beneath the cheeky chap.
Guys like him have put world music on the map.

Yeah! Guys like him make everyone at Womad,
from small children to old grannies, dance and clap.
Right! Ta ta tati tati tap tap tap…
tap tap…(*diminuendo*)…tap…

SHORT CUTS
Home and Away

Tottenham. East Stand. Fade up on an animated foursome,
cold noses and ringed eyes, surreally in working clothes,
his chauffeur suit and hat matched neatly
with her care-home matron's uniform;
a redhaired daughter's renal unit overalls offset
by young son's A&R man Appalachian look.
Long hold on the family, defined now, in this place,
intently following a small white sphere
outlandishly empowered, through planned shapes and baulks,
to rare goals, near-misses, triumphs and defeats.

Flashback. Argentinean with prophet's beard
weaves a path through lame defenders
as the mother-yet-to-be leaves home, stunted, unloved,
for a mousehole in Tulse Hill, swallows packs of Paracetamol,
and waits in Mayday for electrocution.
Down disinfected halls she meets a hopeful cabbie,
practising the knowledge like prayers,
primal fears so focused on his bladder,
facing journeys, he drives only round the bend.
Nelson plagued with sea-sickness, and Nightingale fatigue,
they rise to take their crosses, marry after weeks,
with what prospects only they foresee;
they talk so stiltedly and hug like clipboards.
But fate has settled they will be suburban pioneers.
All they need now is to find the spot.

Cut to when patrols round B&Q are ambushed
by the cabbie's childhood memories —
on a beer-crate watching Blanchflower —
so the pair fall captive to the force that drills the years.
Paint this in a dream-scene, splayed on the bed —
his palms, not electrodes, pressed against her temples —
every surface strewn with home shirts,
away kits, tickets and programmes.
As she shudders under him, overlap each breath
with birth-pangs, first words, echoes of school playgrounds,

cries of wounds and victories, tomfoolery of feast-days,
footsteps along halls of work, banter in a black cab,
ribald outbursts in the stand — fixed by clips of cup runs,
laced with commentary, struggles up and down.
Climax when their lad comes out as a Wembley mascot.

Cue a second half decline, how luck shifts perceptively.
Close up of the boy's eyes, glittering, inspired,
yet already mirrors of his mother's illness.
Enter through them to another weave of spaces
where the years unfold to hostile chants and handclaps.
Overlay their bitter voices: mistrust, poverty, and grief.
Hold on his father, beaten, head in hands.
Silence for a legend, split by a shrill blast.
Segue through the slow burgeon of recovery
across spare echoes from the training ground,
sounds at home now edged with hard intent
found only in acceptance, the need to change position.
Focus on a full screen Christmas card: self-portrait
in their working gear, faces mud-smeared,
under the new chauffeur's caption: *Well, Shit Happens!*

Endgame: through the mist of White Hart Lane
floodlights infuse the features of thousands;
voices surge in one ironically held note.
Float random words recalled from boyhood annuals,
more sounds than signs: adroit, sublime, indefatigable.
Hone in a last time on the family in the stand,
illumined not by Sunday hacks' puffed prose
but unmediated acts of focus,
faith and ritual that entwine lives
separately unwinding; as they threaten to disintegrate,
lure them to such spaces where these histories
and what is yet to come pass through or collide.
A small passion practised at least twice a week.
Still an object lesson for celestial playmakers:
how simple and well-drilled communion can be.

ALT. FOLK TALE: THE DEMON FIDDLER

All Souls' Night. After hours. Squat session in the old courts.
Drunk and fiddle-player, Molloy sat in a corner
bowing planxties, with a wild-eyed young traveller,
hove-to for the winter, smoking skunk.
Through the haze a desultory fight broke out.
She took him to her room of pagan tapestries
to salve his wounds, and told him of her journeys
in pursuit of happiness, wherever the road turned.
In the small hours he lay naked with her by the embers,
breathless at the unschooled certainty she took him with,
bracelets jangling as she stroked his flanks,
burying his face in dreadlocks full of sandalwood.
And when he should have woken in his wife's dry bed
to hold his children, he still stretched, sweat-soaked,
on her rug in the glow of a new load of pallet-blocks.

They made love secretly through the cold months;
while he played sessions in the city pubs and clubs
she sold rings and pendants beaten out of silver
at the market, and worked on an old diesel bus.
He told her how he feared damnation:
growing older with no memory of pleasure,
stumbling blind along thin corridors of debris
from the edifice he built and day by day destroyed.
As spring came closer, panic set in him.
One evening, steaming rum, he pinned her to the wall
in her backyard – donkey-jacket, oil-stained hands –
and made them fuck like strangers.
Later, in her bed, her gaze on his, she rode him gently.
He thought only of his sleeping wife, his children's skin.
Sigh as they might, their time had passed.

Seasons later, twelve steps to redemption,
carrying his fiddle to a theatre pit
Malloy turned down a Georgian crescent
and saw her at an open window, blowing smoke.
He waived the whiskey, the white line on the table,
but through talk of open roads, other lands and lovers,

tales of sobriety, his longing mocked him:
how to be forgiven if you don't transgress?
Denial flared and scorched his fingers.
When he rose he could not even meet her lips.

Over the grey street she stared from her window
as he disappeared into the near park shadows.
Through the tinder of his thoughts, old fears flamed;
where he had been he could no more recall,
where he travelled now, see only smoke.
He reached the well where legend had St Ann decline,
weeping for the ghost of a black knight.
Once he would have taken out his fiddle and played hell.
But there was no music in him. Leant against the bench,
he drummed his fingers on dead wood.

ON GUARD

The sky disintegrates in off-white cascades;
as crosswinds slam the nursery schoolyard,
ridging debris of bikes, ladders, tunnels, slides,
dwarf shapes in yellow capes and boots investigate.

One is still, whose habit is to scream for territory,
defy exchange, tilting for certainties
as he feeds streams of mucus,
three-fingered, nose to mouth.

Sentry by the giant pencil,
eyelids, lips and cheeks touched
by melting flakes, when he is sure, he turns,
makes new prints on the spangled sheet,

meets you with whirling eyes
and, in case you forget, says: blizzard —
so the swirling moment's fixed
where he can scan it, prepossessed.

Who are you to tell him, as he learns his art,
what the years may wreak on him,
how constant the vigil,
the search for harder terms?

This is infancy. It has benefits.
He stands apart. You watch him,
through the frozen air.
He walks into your heart.

MR O'REGAN CALLS TIME

Your time comes to leave.
It seems a waste to me.
If your time comes at all
let it stay at least a while,
have some cake and eat it,
gather rosebuds, dance a reel,
get wasted for good reason,
save stitches and sing songs.

Yet, for old times' sake,
you face a kind of exit,
and you have to take it.
So you leave loose crumbs,
stained skins, cut threads,
the echo of kicked heels,
dying voices locked in,
no more to belong.

I say, take your time,
take it in both hands,
give thanks for it.
Savour how it tasted
as it stretched and turned.
And when it comes,
as it must again, remember
how it is, now and then.

ARTFUL DODGER

The grandfather as tramp, stained fingers
locked on the handle of his pram,
some fancy in you grips, and childhood spent,
you introduce yourself to countless squats,
books like curious visitors in your pockets,
park mud stuck to your boots;
pursuing his laconic ghost
detoured into dole offices,
too sharp to miss the first path back
to the not-so-open road of rhetoric,
the rhythmic train of vagrant thoughts.

Any kind of ship that sails you jump,
leave women who would carry you,
children you should hold;
hands-on grip of thumb and finger
best used ferrying material along clear lines;
raising chasers; curled into a fist;
or on dull afternoons hung-over,
stabbing notes on entries
to your stapled magazine
as worn boots walk you in tight circles,
the whore muse talks you deep into a hole.

Boy-faced, blue-eyed and cocksure
it seems the years have spared you,
but the truth peddles in wear and tear;
for each pioneer thinking his path unique,
jokers without number walk this way.
So now some God's eye camera hones in
from humming spheres to pinprick figure,
stranded at your own news-stand, stained fingers
and laconic calls — *Read All About It*;
how the child obsessed with vagabonds and pirates
slowly turns into the man possessing nothing
when the Devil comes to trade.

RABBIT
Composition: Describe One of Your Pets

At first my mother thought the lionhead Rex a good idea.
He moved into the hutch under the stairs,
lay on laps with pert grey ears, thumped on cue,
ate well. I called him Ruff.

But he saw the whole house
as his hunting ground, four floors and an attic,
flippeting upstairs to scrape and tear
all covered surfaces then disappear.

She might have worn it but for the deposits,
mostly on her pillow. She told me
he would stop when he was done. But it was more
a matter of possession than real sex.

When her family stayed over
Ruff was sentenced to the study. It became a habit.
Once his charges at the door died down
he hid under the chair, turned wild.

Black eyes peered from the shadow.
Reach to take him on sabbatical
downstairs, he gouged your hand
or bit into the soft flesh of your arm.

Put back in his shed at night he rattled
his water bottle with his teeth.
In his cell he started to eat paperbacks;
on a dirty protest, sprayed the desk.

Well-kept rabbits span ten years:
grooming, potholing, real sex.
On excursions he sat still in the hall,
stared morosely, and refused to feed.

After work my mother took him
to be seen again. But he did not return.
A tumour, spread from jaw to brain
had eaten half his palate.

My mother toured the floors
of torn carpets, scarred wallpaper,
pale stains, and whispered,
'It was our home, or him.'

I know the lionhead Rex was a mistake now.
What he craved he was denied, what festered in him
learnt how to destroy. I miss him. So he made his mark.
Other issues in this house can't be put down.

NIGHTLIGHTS

Closing time. They gather in their lower ground floor,
with patio graced by clay muses, to watch each other's faces
deepen in candlelight, take enough wine
to loosen tongues tied by bland days,
become heroes among taramasalata and garlic bread.

The volume rises; enthusiasms eddy round Palestrina;
laughter ripples as motley caps come out of briefcases,
or stop doubling as oven cloths.

Past two — more hallucinatory than they could dream of,
sputtering light refracts from curved glasses
tilted towards clipped beards and pursed lips,
spectacles and earrings. One voice echoes another
along carefully alliterated lines.
Masks melt and set, set and melt,
as they make believe their illuminations
penetrate and reveal so much.

So who should tell them, while at last they search for coats,
they could be train-spotters in a night café,
terrace-fodder on the buffet car home;
a mastery of signs means no more than the love
of number plates, or memories of a perfectly weighted pass?
As if they don't already know, when night air pierces
the glow of arrogance, this is another season —
and, truth be told, more Blackpool than Rimbaud.

MRS MOLLOY

After Molloy's gig, when he trips through jigs and ballads
and the band call her on stage, in a green shawl
to dance a ponderous reel,
he steps down, swaggers to the bar,
towelling sweat; loudmouthed and flushed,
she tosses her lush hair;
they pose with arms linked and lips pursed
for toasts and photographs acclaiming fifteen years.

But slapped by the night air
they must parade alone, lost to the *craic*,
through shades of false paths taken, passages to come;
she baulked by others borne to hidden beds,
he by the sheer weight of her dregs.
When she stumbles, takes his arm,
and cries 'Ach well!', he seems to shrink
as if still stage-struck by the part he plays.

Cowped in the dark of the children's room
she cradles a bottle slipped from a drawer,
singing *The Blacksmith* as they sleep.
He lies naked in the iron bed,
waiting till she reels in and lets him strip her,
eyes closed to the body they have left her;
and they roll on the stained floor together
where they fought once, through love of metaphor.

The last word is hers. On the sheet once more
her eyes search his face so their gaze meets
grained with stale lust and sorrow,
lost when he turns from her.
Listening to her sleep, he mutters in the dark —
struck, among the stills that mark their song and dance,
how one look only captures what's become of them —
happy anniversary, *a stór mo chroí…*

S.O.S.

Flynn hates hospitals. Yet he haunts them.
So to Observation, and Clare Tom.
Flynn scrolls through years, busking in Antibes,
robbed under the Acropolis,
arguing on slip-roads from Berlin to Damascus
till the fork comes, takes him home,
but leaves Tom sitting in bleak rooms
toping and drawing the same views.
While Flynn dreams him stranded on black rocks
he punctuates his life with bottles
holding messages sent only to himself.

Some go astray. So here lies Tom in a dry bed,
bruised from falls, docked in a red wool hat,
snagged jumpers strewn over his cover,
stuttering and shaking on a Valium drip,
beached only since his legs have given up.
Flynn cuts his omelette, and spoons jelly,
steadies his milk, tells him he is safe.
Tom fears creatures in the midnight garden
through his curtain; how to pay this hotel bill
before doormen round the corner beat him —
dabbing his wet cheeks with a frayed sleeve.

So when Flynn leaves him muttering
and fiddling with his line, in bleached
corridors where bland signs point
to acute memories — split flesh and bone,
Caesarean, malignant growth —
lost spirits grill him: is faith here
the butt of nature's mordant jokes,
blight and demon dancing in the blood?
Or is the joker overcome? Quickening, Flynn murmurs:
ask the midnight creatures, doormen at the corner.
Mark what happens to Clare Tom.

PARK LIFE

Sunday, hot late afternoon. Over the park slope
skeins of haze, weed and griddle smoke
drift from clusters of creased cotton, stretched limbs,
stained plates and bottles; strains of laughter
and child's play beckon us towards the past,
but we climb slowly to a clear space,
jousting over boundaries, as these years we must.

May has yet to grasp the frisbee art:
as often as it soars east or west, it falls flat
between us, or she snatches at the air.
Instead of a honed weave of rhythm and arc
we scatter at random, shrugging and sighing.
When she sets off to the sunken willow
I watch her, vexed, in love, at a loss.

Her shock runs like a line to my gut.
On their own half-hidden island of long grass
marked by cans, torn packs and doss-bags,
a tanned figure — coarse beard, glazed eyes —
pins another, sallow legs splayed wide,
arching and dragging; where her smock rides,
pearled hair and swelled flesh sign it is no prelude.

My daughter glances, and again half-looks;
years measured by hamster wheels,
giddy chases and stamped feet, skid to a halt;
all talk of lips bruised by braces
where keen hands are fit to rest,
screen scenes of simulation, are eclipsed
in moments she will and will not forget.

I bend into the insect-laden arc
of sweat, patchouli and stale booze
to fetch the disc, and curse them.
I don't linger, but take us to the play-park
at the far side of the lake
wishing, in the hour before sunset,
we'd stayed in the back-yard to play chess.

RESURRECTION REEL

Good Friday; half a dozen
lost souls locked in
at the Wild Geese;
pints of stout,
loose tongues,
free hands.

MacDonagh — with red cheeks
and archaically long hair —
warmed to the book
he swore he still had in him
on his forebears
and the Easter Rising.

Jabbing a finger
to press home a point
he seemed to tumble forward,
tilted back, searched
for equilibrium, but missed,
fell like a skittle, and lay still.

They bent over him
and feared the worst.
But opening one eye
he rose again in humour,
among friends, too pissed
to think what he had said.

So they broke into song;
it was not till they had ploughed
The Rocks Of Bawn, and run wild
with *The Boys Of Barr na Sráide,*
that any man there even dreamed
of going to his bed.

HERPES VARIATIONS

Form had it they were aiming
for the isthmus under the bushy plain
to make camp — after bizarre journeys
when the whole promontory seemed to rise and fall —
under a vital ridge, to spring out at dawn
with a volley of shots and blades.

But somewhere they took the wrong track
and found themselves in lines
of a major army, some way
from their destination, massed instead
by the back of rolling hills
along the flanks of starched land.

This was no guerrilla sortie:
the battlefield became
a hive of craters, trenches,
nerve, sinew cracked and twisted,
heads broken, flesh blistered —
until, down unseen arteries
a chemical armoury intervened;
all insurgents were contained.

War lasted at least ten days.
Victory was bound to be pyrrhic,
acres left ugly and desolate:
the full toll of resistance.
Now, at the going down of the sun,
the companies of the dead's names echo:
simplex one and two, zoster, cytomegalo.
We will remember them. Amen.

FRINGE THEATRE

One more deftly timed device
of block and line, played out
to a posse over a pub jukebox,
and you come-to in the bar below,
drinking with an old lover,
as if tasting some lost licence
will assuage the emptiness
that hits you, after all the hours
locked in leave your thirst un-slaked.

Home again, you close your front door,
hesitate among unsold prints
too familiar to pierce their mounts.
Upstairs, children slumber at all angles
while in your bed their father mumbles.
You tread landing and hallway
handling evidence of years' work
until dour thoughts of classrooms
end your tour at the wine-rack.

If another bore these gifts
you would cherish every act
or brush-stroke that she made.
But to lay a sodden blanket
over fires within so sorely fails
you burn, as if seeking a lost twin;
anxious for a few lines even in the press
to prove she exists. Like this, in time,
you will be consumed. You have all it takes.

GODFATHER

Iain, you should go.
Get on the damn plane
and hawk in over the
mountains of Switzerland.

Take a taxi and start
spouting French.
Trip up the steps
hammer the doorbell

and when they stand back
gasping, walk in
and kiss his wife
with a maniacal grin.

You want to see his new son.
Make a mark on his world.
Be the first friend who left
everything to play with him.

TRUST PROPERTY

As builders set up in the backyard —
ladders, lunar suits and power hoses —
we leave for the Weald;
I, at the wheel intent on distances,
he, tapping a way through shadows
as if issues riddling the surface
hold us together in this hour,
when what binds us lies unseen,
rooted among sheets and secrets,
children's lives, last night's dreams.

It drives us to these antique homes,
a stubborn woman nursing scars,
the brooding one she holds and fears;
too young to disappear easily
among anoraks and flasks,
but so tired of the days' toll
we search out every edifice
where split histories
and weaknesses we have passed on
we trade for the substance of the dead.

Strange bedfellows it brings: deranged monarchs,
conspirators, soldiers of all faiths,
makers and shifters, ghosts of idle rich.
Now, past ivy-bitten flanks, we steal
through chambers of a storyteller
whose pale imprints under glass spread still,
animated, across continents;
while in these hushed, distempered rooms
he ghosts through narratives he cannot master.
Among grief and fury, velvet and mahogany,
we take time to trespass in his heart.

Nothing happens, nor is it meant to,
yet through each open sense we absorb
what is left here, and transform.
So when we return to our own walls

(scribbled inventory 'all ivery removed'
although striations pierce the plaster still)
not subjects of ourselves, but ciphers now,
we stand with a kind of drunkenness
in the dense plot that holds us here;
laugh, and celebrate where we belong.

TALKING CURE

If he could decide
he would decide
and that decision free him.

Only for the next barbed hook;
to be reeled in
and left to toss

on the grey slab,
thirsting for another
svelte leap free;

shear points
in his head again,
wastes of stone.

Caught is caught.
On and on.
Let him dream.

SEEING THINGS THROUGH
Sunt lachrimae rerum

Expectation fails.
As if what's said could intercede.
It's only ourselves, in the living room
of my old house, where we gather
when our fabric perishes or grows
and we must realign interiors,
architects of all that's left to us.

It happens unseen and unheard
between hand movements, checks of eyes,
working, and worked on by silence.
Karaoke in the Grand Hotel,
shows where celebrities trade
backstage passes for photo-opportunities,
skydives and half-marathons, are now memories.

This is my grand-niece, her eleventh birthday.
She reclines, pink-smocked, in my armchair —
sore tracks, shot gums, thin white hair —
salt pressed on her fingertips to lick
as we clear plates of homemade cake,
trade in common stock, strive to avoid
pitfalls, and dig ourselves out.

She is half-lost already,
protocol abandoned,
slipping back, unhealed.
I dare not touch her till she leaves
slung on her mother's shoulder,
but, lips pressed on her brow,
I feel how she is hollowed —

while the woman leant into my arms,
head heavy with sorrow,
fills this exit,
braced against vigils,
and beyond, long years to rebuild,

trailing her own mother, leaden-eyed,
her pallid brother, cracking jokes.

Our visitors leave.
We, who live here,
turn circles, missing what they take,
to claim back what is ours.
It may seem we lose hope.
But this is our design.
Memory will not fail.

LITTLE MAL
After Raymond Carver

Friday afternoon, I meet my friend.
We don't hunt game or fish the goddam river.
We shoot bar-billiards in the Free Butt.
This is a man I can play with,
ambitions measured by contours on walking-maps,
the negotiation of shopping lists.
He tackles hours indoors growing wheatgerm,
studying train magazines, works hard at his handicap.

Home is where an older woman shares benefits.
When times are safe she sets tasks
with stepladders, Stanley knives and mastic.
On couch days he does nothing
but lie still to cheat the kiss of fears.
Each brand of medication takes him weaving
through side-effects to the same place.
Talking brains, a gap is a gap.

We come here to exchange accounts
over the baize-topped box with mushrooms.
But it is no match. When he is struck
I can only sit and watch.
His neck stiffens, his eyes lock.
He has time to whisper before
he slips and judders through internal exits;
bad breaks wiped as he hits the black.

Yet, for us, the game is enough.
He drifts back, checking his watch,
searching the contents of his wallet.
I slide the nipples on the board to nought.
In the aftermath we don't shake hands,
we hold them. And when the bar drops
we scatter the balls we are left with,
have another pint, and laugh.

MOLLOY'S CHRISTMAS MESSAGE

You will get nothing out of me this year.
So consider a less hallowed mother,
and her journey, in a spirit of goodwill.

Of three brothers who set out to seek their fortune,
the eldest, on a cursed bi-polar expedition
through war-torn and incestuous streets,
disappeared into darkness,
five years, to the day,
before our daughter's birth.

Haunted by his loss, one they called the wain
with piercings, tricoloured Mohican,
and his first trackmarks, loyally went after him
from the balcony of a tower block.
The evening of our son's first birthday, in December.
Jokes, at the wake, about pieces on earth.

Ten years after, the busker on tin whistle
who escaped, tells her from a far-flung pay-phone
cancer in his lung has conquered the ascent
to his brain, and travelled all his bones.
Hope must not be given up. Local healthcare,
where his hat hangs, is second to none.

She is drowning her sorrows,
as if they weren't already sodden,
and may soon follow.

Forgive me then if I am loath to offer
compliments of a season
when it seems more probable
God Almighty impregnated a wee virgin,
our saviour was born among piles of dung
later to hang on his own cross.

We can still sing alleluia. Unto us
a son is given. In spite of his best efforts,
more keep getting taken.

SOFT TERRITORY

At the rump of the near-bankrupt store
past soft furnishings and bedroom suites
they meet weekly for a light lunch.

In kits of cashmere and coiffures
they raise the arched look, cocked coffee cups,
pursed lips, knives slid between toast flaps,
as barricades against thoughts of faces cracked,
bulging joints, emergency plumbers and plasterers,
the unthinkable.

            It is soft territory,
where no one's possessions mimic their own totems,
hard news borne to them by wires
whistling over winter streets
translate into comfortable anecdotes;
like hours wasted in bleached corridors
waiting for the mercy of consultants
who operate like hauliers on a hinterland,
some tickets marked return, some not.

Their ache for tenderness,
dark troughs, untreatable regrets,
they will no more discuss.
They work with the muted adrenalin of rehearsal
for the feared theatre is close.
They know that when their bent forms shuffle off
in hats and coats, the tables will be cleared,
and bright-eyed women who have tea after
antenatal classes take their place.

FLYNN'S CHRISTMAS LIST

I address this to dear old Doctor Bermingham
who always asked after my mother,
prescribed the company of dogs, and caught pneumonia,
the keen new psychiatrist from Saudi Arabia,
or any other who might want to put on
a red suit and try out a few belly-laughs.

Don't bring medication that means parched lips,
hallucinations, delayed impact, or no thrust;
slow-release capsules that interact
with cheese and herring in fatal detonations;
or learned papers on the biochemistry of disorder;
how a minority fail to respond to invading forces
like renegades in a hill-fort surrounded by tanks and mortars
determined to hold out for the dark cause.

Please substitute a simpler expedient,
in the name of goodwill and peace on earth:
a sense of time that passes on a well-paced linear path
where the loved remain in the heart
and we are this evening who we were this morning.
This has a name, but I forget.

I understand if it's too much.
Keep me the Perry Como album,
It's A Wonderful Life, a half-
-bottle of Southern Comfort, a bag
of pistachio nuts. Biscuits and brandy
are on the willow-patterned plate in the hearth.
The chimney was swept last week
by the new-age tree surgeon across the street.

I can't promise to be asleep,
but I can fake it.
I'm sorry if the need to be good has been lost
in the effort to be perfect;
and for doubting you exist.
I write this in the hope you will not forget.

TRACKS

Here are the dark woods and deep snows
lining ridges and silent heavy branches.
There the frozen lake stretches north
along the line reckless pioneers take.
Lame old man, I have to watch them leave,
rock here, with my weak heart.

I know what they seek, these pale ones,
setting off with deep loads in haste
as if they become heroes
travelling a wilderness of white and brown.
I have been where their journeys end:
a waste where whey-faced youths

strain their dogs to strike back through
the wild, with no strength to move.
Flying from a bland world and its sorrows
won't turn their lost lives into legends.
Sharp-bitten, swallowed by deep drifts,
only mournful howls will be heard of them.

KISS ME HARDY

Sea fret spurs from the shore,
swirls over scrub paths on Race Hill.
Piecemeal, the city is obscured;
but lost in his own wreaths,
walking from gray blocks to the west —
locked windows, fire-escapes in nets —
the bowed man notes only a quick chill
like commentary and grandstand thrum
heard vaguely over sentry voices in his skull.

Yet where chalk track meets tarmac
carpeted in fake turf, and the course fence forks,
among insurgent shafts of sun
he is attacked — a sudden cavalcade
of spangled vests, caps, goggles, gleaming bits
and bridles, leather whips and saddles,
silken flesh that springs and stretches,
manes and tails flying, hooves hammering,
scatters his dark guard and streaks through him —

kicking up the past, raising ghosts
of fest and pageant, sport of kings and gangs,
exiting as fast to what cannot be seen.
Spared a moment's stalls and nets inside,
he glances coastward, while lost larks sing
over him, at the immense dance
of wrack, sun and edifice,
and laughs: for, whatever blinds him, still
he is a man who notices such things.

GROOMBRIDGE

Among stifling stone on a summer afternoon
we pay lip service to the formal gardens,
clipped hedges, moats, life-size chess-pieces,
and duly visit the mock study of the writer
in late residence: a staunch, bearded man
still sharpening his quills.

But we will not stand in awe.
We come for the barge ride to the forest,
one step from a flaked pontoon
that leads to landscapes pitched by a quick mind
to acres of eccentric paths, grottoes with reed figures,
wigwams, hill-forts, spiral mazes and still pools
mirrored by flickering glass; where the children,
half-naked, discover Arcady, only a day out.

So when we return to the stained walls
and the peacock struts,
rattling, breathless, for his rigid empire,
natives charge at him, whooping
in mock war-paint; he retreats to the slates
with barely the power to lift his rump.

This has become our place: a multitude of trespassers.
Without us, it turns in and decays.
From the worked fields and forests
our echoes and shadows dance
over the cramped ghosts of master and aristocrat.
When we leave, common names
scraped in the driveway disappear, piecemeal,
as another day's footsteps tread past.

MALLOY'S RETREAT

I have come home.
From exiled shores
in steps retraced
along thin high-hedged lanes,

past Kilbarry, to a smallholding
of strawberries and courgettes
I return to sit alone
with my grand-uncle.

Porter and a peat fire
flickering on his cheeks,
this eager white-haired figure
leans back, piercing years

of songs and scars,
rebel, prisoner,
fierce farmer
harvesting lost fields.

Round his glimmering house
dark Cork hills grow still.
I bow to take his tilting glass,
kiss his sleeping brow, at peace.

TERRAPIN
The Conquest of Happiness — not Russell — Flynn

Crazy Flynn's redeemer is a red-eared terrapin.
His tank sits in the upstairs toilet
on a perfect shelf, with pump and heater,
ultraviolet light, slime-green plastic islet.

Once he suffered from neglect,
when he was rarely cleaned, dried pellets
and uneaten dandelions messed the murky water
while unbroken light made him insomniac.

But his depressed mien prompted reassessment
of his needs. His pump flows freely now
by pale blue stones, he has eight hours' sleep,
eats health-foods from lancefish to bloodworms.

Through his glass, pots of pellet food are stacked
so pictures of his tribe accompany him.
Behind these he plays peek-a-boo,
splashing, bubbling, as he bats and swims.

Sideways movements of a friendly head
invoke a slow dance, shifting weight
from claw to claw; eyes widening
with each rush of being watched.

All other motions, vents, and plumbing work
are witnessed with delight; his shell bangs
on the glass as he shifts for a clear view.
In trance mode he basks under his light

lifting two diagonally opposed feet;
for deep slumber all his fleshy parts
withdraw under his crust in a dark corner
where he dreams of oceans;

or perhaps the dredged lake
(shopping trolleys bared, rubbish bins and bikes)
where he stumped its whole length
to climb to rock-pools, only to be met

by shoals of youths — wondering what it takes
to break a turtle's shell, if he stood on his hind legs,
would he practise Ninja moves, did he hump frogs? —
and left in Flynn's soft hands.

Unlike the regularly dying brood
of rodents, and intrusive cats
this numbskull — dirty mottled shell,
leather limbs, elastic neck striped yellow —

who extends his head in pleasure,
withdraws it in unease, swims expressively,
and will do so after Flynn is dead,
answers all his prayers.

Not to be handled. Expectations minimal.
Boundaries clear, detachment possible.
In the closet without windows is a creature,
not purloined for children, but saved from them.

So to all concerned with liberation
leave him where he is. Back to front on the green toilet,
nodding to his terrapin. Have continents, faiths, wars.
But say goodnight to Flynn. *Goodnight to Flynn.*

ENVOI
The Stowaway's Song

February evening,
Your last day,
The heavy bonds that held you here
Have all been cast away;
No line into your vein now
No glass between your lips,
As you lie licking grains of salt
Pressed upon your fingertips.

Stowaway, drift gently
But drift deep.
All your walking's over now,
This is where you sleep.
Stowaway, drift gently
But drift far.
Let this tide take all you were
Away from all you are.

You must use this craft now
To bear you through the cold,
Hidden with your treasures
In its creaking hold;
These objects you vivify,
Lines you read or sing;
Talismans to testify
To travellers here you cannot bring.

Take this sheath of images,
Garnered year by year,
That mark a quick life's changes
From safe hours to hours of fear.
There is no trace of womanhood,
No print of all you might have made,
But the passage of a childhood
Cut off now, stowed away.

So ride this bright craft
Into the dark tide,
Receding as moments
Pass, keepsakes by your side.
And when you have landed
Step into the risen sun,
Where the trail of all that's ended
Meets the path of all that is begun.